CHINA

Heather DiLorenzo Williams
and Warren Rylands

EYEDISCOVER

Go to **www.eyediscover.com** and enter this book's unique code.

BOOK CODE

AVK88625

EYEDISCOVER brings you optic readalongs that support active learning.

Published by AV² by Weigl
350 5th Avenue, 59th Floor New York, NY 10118
Website: www.eyediscover.com

Library of Congress Control Number: 2018953517

ISBN 978-1-4896-8049-5 (hardcover)

Printed in Brainerd, Minnesota,United States
1 2 3 4 5 6 7 8 9 0 22 21 20 19 18

082018
120917

Project Coordinators: John Willis
Designer: Mandy Christiansen

Weigl acknowledges Alamy, iStock, and Shutterstock as the primary image suppliers for this title.

EYEDISCOVER provides enriched content, optimized for tablet use, that supplements and complements this book. EYEDISCOVER books strive to create inspired learning and engage young minds in a total learning experience.

Watch
Video content brings each page to life.

Browse
Thumbnails make navigation simple.

Read
Follow along with text on the screen.

Listen
Hear each page read aloud.

Your EYEDISCOVER Optic Readalongs come alive with...

Audio
Listen to the entire book read aloud.

Video
High resolution videos turn each spread into an optic readalong.

OPTIMIZED FOR
- TABLETS
- WHITEBOARDS
- COMPUTERS
- AND MUCH MORE!

CHINA

In this book, you will learn about

- where it is
- who lives there
- what it is known for

and much more!

China is a country on the continent of Asia.

6

China is believed to be about 5,000 years old.

China has more people than any other country. More than 1.3 billion people live there.

皮影

10

The capital city of China is called Beijing.

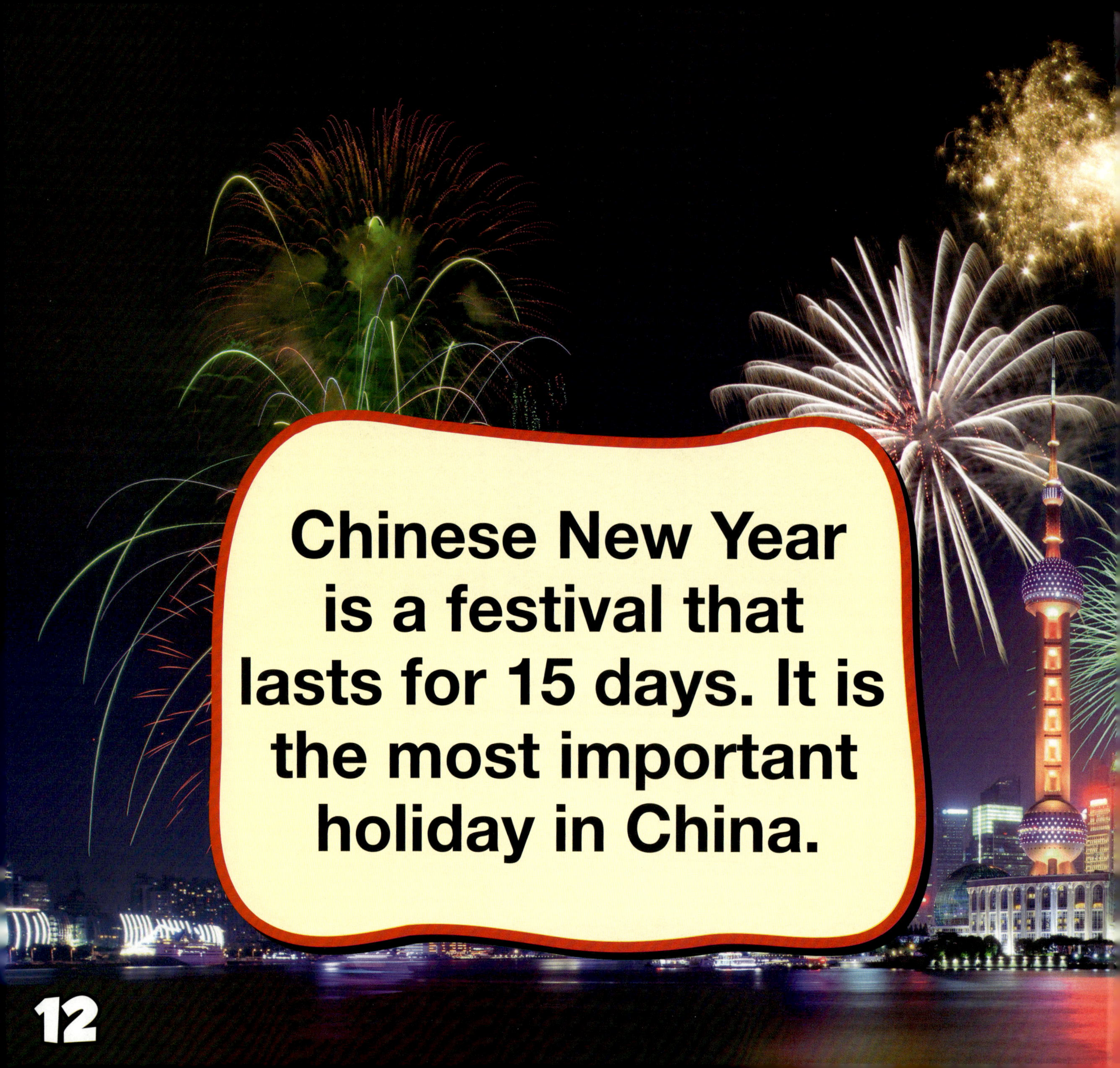

Chinese New Year is a festival that lasts for 15 days. It is the most important holiday in China.

Many people visit the Great Wall of China. It was built to protect China from invaders.

Visitors also come to see the Terracotta Army. These statues were made more than 2,000 years ago.

One national Chinese symbol is the dragon. It is a symbol of good luck for the people of China.

China has many beautiful forests and mountains. Mount Huangshan is known as “the loveliest mountain of China.”

CHINA BY THE NUMBERS

The **Forbidden City** in Beijing is a **palace** with **9,000** rooms.

The **Great Wall of China** is about **2,300 years old.**

There are about **8,000** clay soldiers in the Terracotta Army.

The **Great Wall of China** is **3,915 miles long.**

(6,300 kilometers)

About
1.2 billion
people around the world speak a form of **Chinese** as their first language.

Beijing has had **15 other names** since it was first founded.

KEY WORDS

Research has shown that as much as 65 percent of all written material published in English is made up of 300 words. These 300 words cannot be taught using pictures or learned by sounding them out. They must be recognized by sight. This book contains 42 common sight words to help young readers improve their reading fluency and comprehension. This book also teaches young readers several important content words, such as proper nouns. These words are paired with pictures to aid in learning and improve understanding.

Page	Sight Words First Appearance
4	a, country, is, of, on, the
7	about, be, old, to, years
8	any, has, live, more, other, people, than, there
11	city
12	for, important, in, it, most, new, that
14	from, great, many, was
16	also, come, made, see, these, were
18	good, one
21	and, as, mountains

Page	Content Words First Appearance
4	Asia, China, continent, country
11	Beijing, capital
12	Chinese New Year, holiday, festival
14	Great Wall, invaders
16	statues, Terracotta Army, visitors
18	dragon, luck, symbol
21	forests, mountains, Mount Huangshan

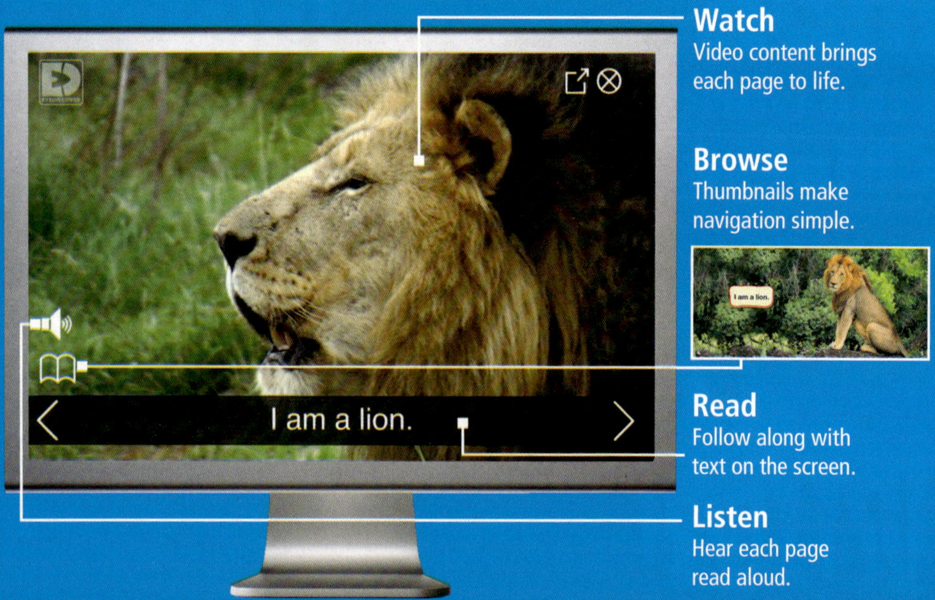

EYEDISCOVER

Go to www.eyediscover.com and enter this book's unique code.

BOOK CODE

AVK88625